Dunamis Children's
DEVOTIONALS

Who Is Jesus

Dunamis Children's
DEVOTIONALS

This Devotional Belongs To:

_____

Copyright

Dunamis Children's DEVOTIONALS

Dedication

I dedicate this devotional to my Lord and Savior, Jesus Christ, for blessing me with the gift of writing and the calling to teach His Word.

To my loving husband, LaDarian Prioleau, and our amazing children, Journee and Landen—thank you for walking with me as we grow together in faith.

And to every parent who desires to raise their children in the truth of God's Word—this is for you. May you be encouraged as you nurture Kingdom disciples in your home.

To every parent who desires to raise their children in the truth of God's Word—this is for you.

Tanicia

www.rempublish.com

Introduction

Welcome!

We created these devotionals with you and your children in mind. In today's society, equipping our children with the truth of God's word is essential. The devotionals provided will help your children understand God's word more practically. May these teachings be a blessing!

Proverbs 22:6 Train up a child in the way he should go: and when he is old, he will not depart from it.

- Read the devotional and scripture.
- Ask your children the questions provided (this is good for reading and comprehension).
- End each devotional with the provided prayer
- Begin to apply the practical application

Recommended Reading Outline

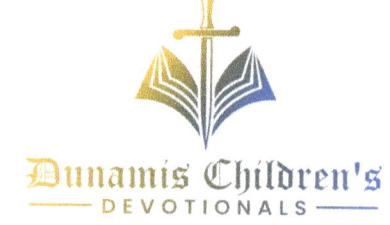

TABLE OF
CONTENTS

Jesus The Son Of God/ Immanuel

Begotten

"The only Son of God," Jesus is the Son of God in a sense that no others are. His divine nature gives him a unique relationship with the Father.

Sin

An offense/wrongdoing against religious or moral law.

Freedom

Liberty from slavery or restrain from the power of another (before we are born again, we were slaves to sin).

9

Jesus The Son Of God/ Immanuel

Read Matthew 1:21-23 AMP

Jesus is the Son of God; he is the only begotten of the Father. He is also Immanuel, "God with us," which means he isn't only the Son of God, but he is also GOD, the Son. This is excellent news; he understands how it feels not to have A good day or when we aren't feeling well. Jesus knows and understands us. God sent Jesus into the world so that we can be free from sin, wrong thinking, and bad influences. Isn't that great news? Jesus came to set us free!

Do you know what it means to be set free? To be "set free" means we now have freedom and liberty to live according to God's word. How exciting! Jesus is always near, open, and willing to hear our prayers; we can talk to him anytime.

Jesus The Son Of God/ Immanuel

Prayer

Would you like to be set free?
If so, repeat this simple prayer after me.

Heavenly Father, I thank you for
sending your son Jesus into the world
to save me from my sins.

Please help me live my life in
obedience to your word and follow
you all of my days in Jesus' name.
Amen.

Practical Application

Remember that Jesus is always available to hear your prayers in your daily activities. He can relate to you and help you when you're struggling. Jesus also suffered and endured temptation, just like you. As it says in Hebrews 2:18, He can set you free!

_____

_____

_____

_____

_____

_____

_____

_____

_____

REVIEW

What does the name "Jesus" mean?

_____

_____

_____

_____

Circle One: True or False:

Jesus came to save his people from their sin.

Can you think of something you need freedom from? (Use this time to discuss)

_____

_____

_____

_____

_____

_____

_____

_____

JESUS THE SON OF GOD WORD SEARCH

JESUS THE SON OF GOD

Circle the words listed below.

```
I R S O N M I U G X
M F M O T N M O E L
R Q J F N X M N Q B
V V A R R F A K C B
U Y Z E S I N K H W
F M Z E G U U W V J
Q T D D O G E G Z B
T K M O O I L G O D
Y C D M J E S U S S
I G V Z F P U Y W Z
```

Jesus	Son	Immanuel
God	Sin	Freedom

14

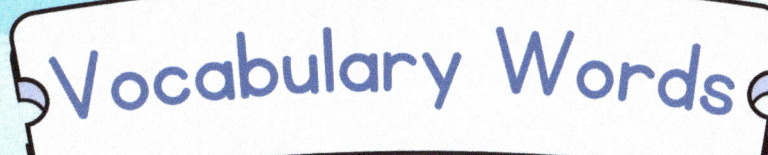

Vocabulary Words

Jesus, Our Deliverer

Deliverer

One who delivers, rescues, or sets free, a savior or preserver.

To Save

To deliver from sin, to rescue or deliver from danger or harm

Jesus, Our Deliverer

Read: Matthew 8:1-4 KJV

Acts 2:21 KJV 'And it shall come to pass, that whosoever shall call on the name of the Lord shall be saved. '

Jesus is our deliverer. To deliver means "to rescue or set free." In the scripture above, the man in the story was sick, and when Jesus stretched forth his hand, he could make him clean. Jesus set him free from sickness. Friends, have you ever had An upset tummy after eating too many yummy sweets? Whenever we aren't feeling well, we can pray to Jesus, remember he hears our prayers, and just as he delivered the leper man of his sickness, he will do the same for you and me.

Jesus, Our Deliverer

Jesus wants to save us, which means he desires to deliver us from our sins and bad habits. When Jesus saves us, he also protects us from injury or harm. As we have learned from the scripture, whenever we call on the name of the Lord Jesus Christ, we will be saved. This is wonderful news: we do not have to face injury or harm alone. Jesus is always willing to save us; we simply need to call on His name!

Jesus, Our Deliverer

Prayer

Jesus, thank you for being our savior and deliverer. I also thank you that we can be protected from harm and injury when we call on your name. Lord Jesus, please preserve and protect me all the days of my life. In Jesus's name, AMEN!

Practical Application

Remember that Jesus is always near you. He is willing and able to protect you from evil and keep you safe from harm. Think of a time when you felt protected and remember that it is Jesus who safeguards and redeems you!

_____

_____

_____

_____

_____

_____

_____

_____

_____

REVIEW

Fill in the Blank:

Jesus is our _____

What happens when Jesus saves us?

_____

_____

_____

_____

_____

Circle One:

True or False: Jesus set the leper man free from his sickness.

Jesus, Our Deliverer
Activity
Word Scramble:

Word Scramble

Put your puzzle solving skills to the test with our word scramble

Look carefully at the jumbled words and try unscrambling as many as you can.

eelivDr _____   Saev _____   Set Feer _____

yraPer _____   sesuJ _____   Svaior _____

Answer Key

Look carefully at the jumbled words and try unscrambling as many as you can.

eelivDr **Deliver**   Saev **Save**   Set Feer **Set Free**

yraPer **Prayer**   sesuJ **Jesus**   Svaior **Savior**

Vocabulary Words

Jesus, Our Shepherd

Shepherd

Jesus, the good shepherd who knows his sheep.

Sheep

Sheep are those who are followers of the good shepherd, Jesus.

Jesus, Our Shepherd

John 10:11 I am the Good Shepherd. The Good Shepherd lays down His [own] life for the sheep.

Jesus is our Good Shepherd; He laid down His life for you and me. Jesus cared for us so deeply that He willingly sacrificed Himself. Because Jesus laid down His life for us, He is an excellent example of a selfless servant. Do you know what a shepherd is?

A shepherd tends to and guides sheep. Do you know who Jesus' sheep are? If you said we are the sheep, you are correct. Like sheep, we are meant to be guided and cared for by Jesus.

Jesus will lead and guide us along the right path; He will never leave or forsake us. As our Shepherd, He will provide for us, and we can trust Him. Friends, Jesus desires to lead us down the righteous path. He will be with you in times of darkness and help you when you feel afraid. The sheep of Jesus will hear His voice and follow Him alone.

Are you one of Jesus's sheep? Do you hear his voice? Let's Pray!

Jesus, Our Shepherd

Prayer

Heavenly Father, thank You for sending Your Son, Jesus, my Good Shepherd. Thank You, Lord Jesus, for laying down Your life for me. Please guide, protect, and be with me in my dark and light times. In Jesus's name, I pray, Amen!

Practical Application

Read Psalm 23 to see how the Lord is your good Shepherd. He is with you in your darkest times and is always by your side. God is here to guide, care for, and protect you as His sheep.

Psalm 23:1 The LORD is my Shepherd [to feed, to guide and to shield me], I shall not want.

_____

_____

_____

_____

_____

_____

_____

_____

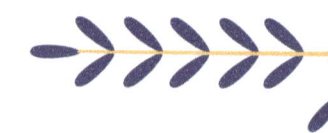

Jesus, Our Shepherd
Coloring Activity Sheet

Jesus is my Good Shepherd!

Jesus, Our Good Shepherd (Poem)
Written by Tanicia Prioleau

Jesus is our good shepherd, gentle and true. He laid down His life, and He cares for you.

His voice is a whisper that calls us to stay. We'll follow Him closely and never go astray.
When He comes again, the heavens will roar, A promise of joy as we reach heaven's door.
In pastures of plenty, He leads us each day, Providing our needs in His loving way.

No one like Him can ever compare. So let's learn of His kindness and show Him we care. His arms are wide open, ready to hold us tight.

With many mansions waiting in the bright light, we'll gather together in His grace and delight. Let's seek Him with gladness while there's time to find. Our good shepherd leads with a heart so kind. So thank you, dear Jesus, for all You do, our faithful protector. We'll always love You!

Vocabulary Words

Jesus, The Captain of our Salvation

Captain

The commander of a unit or a body of troops (we are part of the body of Christ)

Provision

The fact or state of being prepared beforehand.

Salvation

Deliverance from the power and effects of sin.

Jesus, The Captain of our Salvation

Hebrews 2:10 For it became him, for whom are all things, and by whom are all things, in bringing many sons unto glory, to make the captain of their salvation perfect through sufferings.

Jesus is the captain of our salvation, which also means he is considered the champion/originator of our salvation. He made the required provisions so that we can follow him and walk by faith. As we learned earlier (in Jesus as our Shepherd), we know Jesus is a good leader.

Since Jesus is the captain of our salvation, we can now accept him and have eternal life with him. This is good news; we now can join the cool ship of salvation, and guess what...... We have the best captain ever! JESUS

Friends, it is good to have leadership qualities like Jesus; we want to be champions in everything we do. Let us pray!

Jesus, The Captain of our Salvation

Prayer

Heavenly Father, I thank You for Your dear Son, JESUS Christ. Lord Jesus, I am grateful for you being the captain of my salvation; I know that You will always guide me down the right path. Thank You for all that You've done and will continue to do. Help me to follow You all the days, of my life in Jesus' name, AMEN!

Read Hebrews 2 and learn about Jesus as our captain. Think about how to be a leader among your friends. Lead by example—demonstrate kindness, integrity, and strong faith in your actions. Write your thoughts below!

_____

_____

_____

_____

_____

_____

_____

_____

_____

Vocabulary

Jesus, Our Intercessor

Prayer

Prayer is talking to God the Father, through Jesus Christ the Son, by the power of the Holy Spirit.

Intercession

The act of praying on behalf of others. When we pray for others it is a selfless act.

Jesus, Our Intercessor

Hebrews 7:25 Wherefore he is able also to save them to the uttermost that come unto God by him, seeing he ever liveth to make intercession for them.

Jesus forever lives to pray for you and me; the Bible calls Jesus our intercessor. An intercessor is someone who prays for someone else.

Friends, have you ever prayed for your parents? Have you ever prayed for a friend? Maybe your friend was sad or having a lousy day; when you pray for them, you're doing exactly what Jesus does for us.

It's always good to pray for others; God likes it when we pray for others; he enjoys hearing us pray. Since Jesus is the captain, we will follow him as he leads and shows us how to pray for others. Let's learn to pray for others as Jesus prays for you and me.

34

Jesus, Our Intercessor

Prayer

Heavenly Father, thank you for showing me through your son Jesus how to pray for others. Please teach me how to pray according to your word, and please teach me how to pray for others as well. In Jesus name Amen!

After you read the Lord's Prayer model with the children, make it a daily habit to say a simple prayer for others. This will help the little ones focus their prayers not only on themselves but also for those around them. It's a wonderful act of selflessness.

Jesus, Our Intercessor Lord's Prayer

Matthew 6:9-13,15

"Pray, then, in this way:

'Our Father, who is in heaven, Hallowed be Your name.

Your kingdom come; your will be done on earth as it is in heaven.

Give us this day our daily bread.

And forgive us our debts, as we have forgiven our debtors.

And do not lead us into temptation, but deliver us from evil.

For Yours is the kingdom and the power and the glory forever. Amen.

Children, as you begin to pray, write your personal prayers in the bubble below. You can also start writing your prayers in a journal. Remember, God loves to hear us pray.

My Prayers

My Prayers

My Prayers

My Prayers

My Prayers

My Prayers

My Prayers

My Prayers

My Prayers

A Final Note

Thank you for joining me and your little one on this journey through God's Word. Sharing these lessons and truths with your family has been a joy.

I pray this devotional has inspired faith and opened the door for deeper conversations between you and your child. May the Lord guide you as you nurture strong and purpose-driven disciples.

Stay encouraged, stay consistent, and keep Jesus at the center.

Tanicia Prioleau

Fanicia Prioleau

Meet The Author

As a mom deeply passionate about writing and sharing the Word of God, I created Dunamis Children's Devotionals through prayer and my personal experiences from teaching my children about Jesus. This mission is very close to my heart, and my goal is for many children to come to know Jesus Christ through these lessons.

UPCOMING SERIES

WWW.REMPUBLISH.COM

THE HOLY SPIRIT

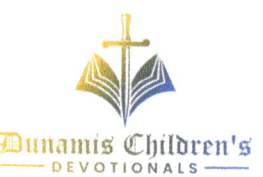

WWW.REMPUBLISH.COM

THE SELFLESS LOVE OF GOD OUR FATHER

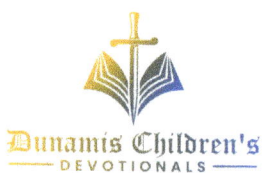

WWW.REMPUBLISH.COM

PROVERBS FOR CHILDREN

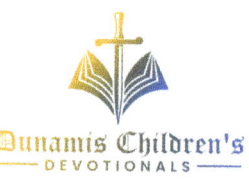

WWW.REMPUBLISH.COM

SAY NO TO FEAR

DID YOU ENJOY THIS DEVOTIONAL? WE WOULD LOVE FOR YOU TO SHARE YOUR FAVORITE PAGE WITH US!

🌐 www.rempublish.com

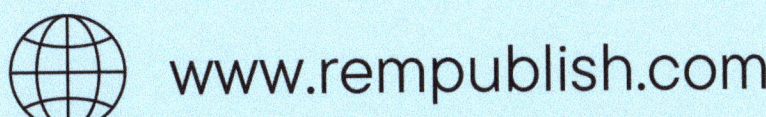 @rempublish

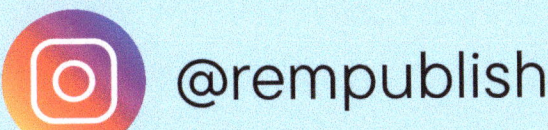 @rempublish

EMAIL US: INFO@REMPUBLISH.COM